Refuge/es

Refuge/es

≈

Michael Broek

Alice James Books

FARMINGTON, MAINE

10 9 8 7 6 5 4 3 2 1

Alice James Books are published by Alice James Poetry Cooperative, Inc.,
an affiliate of the University of Maine at Farmington.

Alice James Books
114 Prescott Street
Farmington, ME 04938
www.alicejamesbooks.org

Library of Congress Cataloging-in-Publication Data
Broek, Michael.
  [Poems. Selections]
  Refuge/es / Michael Broek.
      pages   cm
  ISBN 978-1-938584-12-1 (pbk. : alk. paper)
  I. Title.
  PS3602.R636R46 2015
  811'.6—dc23   2014030176

Alice James Books gratefully acknowledges support from individual donors,
private foundations, the University of Maine at Farmington, and the National
Endowment for the Arts.

ART WORKS.
arts.gov

Cover Art: "Untitled," linoleum cut by Helen Bryant.

CONTENTS

ACKNOWLEDGMENTS

Many of these poems first appeared, often under different titles, in *The American Poetry Review, Beloit Poetry Journal, Connotation Press: An Online Artifact, Exit Strata, Gathered: Contemporary Quaker Poets* (Sundress Publications, 2013), *Great River Review, Literary Imagination, The Literary Review,* and *MiPOesias.*

A selection of poems from "The IED" was published in the chapbook *The Amputation Artist* (ELJ Publications, 2014).

Special appreciation to the editors at *Beloit Poetry Journal,* which published substantial selections from "The Cloud *&* The Counterpane" (summer 2014) and "The Golden Venture" (fall 2014).

As solitary an effort as writing is, this book would not have been possible without the time and guidance of many others. In particular, I would like to thank Peter Murphy and friends at the annual Winter Poetry & Prose Getaway. A scholarship to the Bread Loaf Writers' Conference provided crucial support, and a Fellowship to the MacDowell Colony provided an invaluable safe haven and community in which to revise these poems. For her keen editorial eye, thank you to the ever-intelligent Suzanne Parker, and thank you as well to Carey Salerno and everyone at Alice James Books, especially Julia Bouwsma. Finally, and most profoundly, thank you to my wife, the wonderful writer and poet Laura McCullough, without whose unfailing love, support, and understanding this book would have remained unwritten.

For Peter Broek

≈

Refuge/es

You Are in Another City

Here in my bivouac
on the other side of the world

I will write to you
about all the head-sunk people

eyes bowed thick with fear
walking like statistics up
& down the streets & the ones
who turn their faces

& whom I misbelieve are you.

I am not sure I know the difference anymore
between this person & that
along Kingsland Avenue
though some point guns & others
kiss me hard on the lips
& I am so glad
we are one of those
who point with our mouths
most of the time.

I could say your name
or I could just crawl across your chest
& our thighs would speak the text
lay your head against my neck & come
nameless one
everywhere—

London, Mumbai, New York, Shanghai
these species: citis

this genera: citi
slicing off the—y
          no good asking anyway.

You are in another citi & I
am deep here in myself
less these numbers, less these names & eyes—

but it is the same sky, isn't it…

The Cloud & The Counterpane

In the city I drowned all night in the nothing search for you.

—Ken Chen, from *Juvenilia*

The Cloud 1

citi of never-ending gates
citi of evidence collected in barrels
DNA the hundred-year storm left
waterlogged
along Kingsland Avenue in Greenpoint Brooklyn muck—

citi of Sutton Hoo of golden breast plates
punk teeth false hair

citi of candied orange slices & sushi
that preserved that raw that saturated color
inside the steam-mouthed kitchen

citi of birth
documents floating down to Jersey

citi of preserved women
hanging from fat rafters like antique brooms

citi of preserved men
shut inside glass cases on soft black sheets

citi of gods

citi of devils

citi of can't tell the difference.

The Counterpane 1

Your back
is a constellation
is code map & lexicon
leading the way
across & inside
the counterpane. Time
we have wasted
wanting. This
humming of hands
smoothing
tugging
piecing
palming the skin. Take
the batting. Take
the needle
& sew the
we of us between these

crosswise stitches
mating belly on top
of belly halves:
flax duff
wool tips
cotton waste
& rags.

Whatever it takes to be warm.

Whatever it takes to hold together
two horizons pierced

through with light:

Jacob's Ladder
Flying Geese
Monkey Wrench
Crossroads.
Underground
Railroad quilts
signaling what everyone

desires

kissing—revolution—the gasp—
your hip fastened to mine
unfurled & free.

The Cloud 2

well, there were people not on any maps
but in citis
on the maps

in statistician's shop drawers
shedding citizens' data onto squared
tile floors
& in the server's ever-spooling numbers

circumnavigating solar systems
since numbers
were light
& seemingly infinite

space
& on Tuesday at 5 p.m. the Milky Way is finite
while at 5:01
there is more, *encore du encore du*

in bodega storage closets
& police precinct bathrooms
where there loom broomstick endings

fractions
/
systolic/diastolic

in private club parlors where countries
meet histories written
under invaders' thumbs &

numbers-men gobble tables where eyes are
multipliers
citi's fissures, fissions, fractures

...the ethics of loving are complex
if we can call this loving at all
the 4:05 p.m. from Newark arrives at Penn not at all...

but solidly within dream
nightmare & imagined futures arriving
softly

across bridges leering brightly
in breezeway corners & last-century
elevators

crossing each story's
horizontal steel demarking
each light-pierced foregone life-line

water-line   food-line   power-line
line-up
line of defense

graph paper
the Arecibo message:

11

11

11

11

11

01

11

11

                    OI
                    II
                    OI
                    II
                    IO
                    II
                    II
                    OI
                    X
double-helical human

the extra-terrestrial
signal 6EQUJ5
forward & backward Wow!

The Counterpane 2

The pattern is here.
The shop is mine.
Hour past, hand along
nape of neckline
fabric which
choosing chooses me—
tools:
scissor, machine, spool
blade & rule.

What happened
last night along the roadway
home?

What happened last
star-splintered year
manning the checkpoint?

Or in that secret tree
split open in the garden?

Pattern is here. That
pattern I wasn't meant
to have. Stitches organizing
sky—constellations
pointing toward futures
I didn't know
was there plural.

P=slow loves
    perambulations
    of dresses around the garden
    market flowers
    patterning the day.

Do you have this?
Is there one of these?
What I go finding
is never what I leave
having found—
you.

Dear shopkeeper
stocker &
prophet

I came today
imagining
just where I was going &
you suggested
new ideas.

The Cloud 3

Tal Afar, Iraq
citi of

blood stars
patterning soldiers' boots

splintered windshield
wheeling about Lt.
____'s head

firing the warning
shots

flashing
the hand

signaling
Stop
the Arecibo message

humans
cringing

in the statistician's
office corner

Samar
Hassan
officially unrecorded:

all these blossoming
terrors

& wrapped arms too
sequestered, buried, held

inside chests
inside eyes

mouths groins &
fingers
sliding inside you

kisses
on lips long having

given up
forgetting love:

Samar
beauty
exploding citi

sweet refugee
these are (our) bodies

wet & terrible teeth
marks in flanks

fecund & monstrous
rebar pierced
through the neck, dear

you
dragged under the bush

devoured
meat

which no one loves
no one forgives
everyone forgives

desire

you lover
you citi

absent your —y
devoured

behind the tree in a garden
shadowed
with light

a tree that will outlast
us. man

who has no analog
silly really he has

been in charge for so long.

The Counterpane 3

From one concentric circle to another
span arms

tubes weighed with ink
pinched shut at either end

but pinched or open
splayed from one lip edge to next

arms wrapped under & above
red, blue, green, black

pooled in the elbows
& at each end

a shoulder or a fingertip
edging toward the next circle of voices.

Across a field of cutting grass
stems sighing before the fall

& across the bed
one leveled field touching another

ground panting with
cries. One belly lies atop the other

navels, those circles struck through arms
& legs! arced round.

The Cloud 4

the A to Far Rockaway was bound
to run over Sunando Sen

If I smoked a blunt that day, I wouldn't have pushed him
Menendez said

a universe of subjects
encoded in things

       [a dictatorship

of—(preposition) belonging in, composed
in—(preposition) of perpetuity]

once Blake opened his mouth
*All Sublimity is founded
on Minute Discrimination*

object becoming subject
remaining object

Sunando Sen was bound
to fly when the A to Far Rockaway
arrived.

The Counterpane 4

The only reason rock splits is light
& the only reason our bed at night won't
is luck & determinism
but I can't ever tell the difference, love
so don't ask me any questions.

Priestley on Necessity & Edwards on the Will
provide sound advice on this issue.
In other words & don't tell this to anyone
I have no idea
how the sea may be kept at bay or how

(pieced blue pattern, little genomic ribbon)

this rock split, may be rejoined
except stitching
tonight the light
around your face is daisy

which when mixed with alcohol produces
tinctures for wounds. That this wound
is mine, pay no attention. The world, even
me, will hand you yours.
Then the real nightmares begin.

The Cloud 5

maybe they all
should have died

maybe should I
some choice

left the cartographer
drawing lines

across
citi-maker's lips

blue-veined map
of who is

in charge really
& what a wonderful

elision if
no one.

The Counterpane 5

My head is full of you & the wind
has picked up your scent
bringing you back to me. My head

aches from feeling
& the lights along the sidewalk grow
yellow with their simple being

in the face of all their glassy eyes have seen—
backpacks walking into distance
& shopping carts, carriages & scooters

people too. People not
in citis or on maps—people in each
other's arms. Along the blue-black walkway

beside benches crying with sweat
are her & him & dogs
tethered to their masters

sometimes many in the hands of one
walking with his head down.
In my brain today is hurt

I had not known I wanted & wouldn't
give up. I had finished the quilt
so I went down & sat by the smell-less river—

just a frosted gray strip of moon
laid down between citis that see
each other across the river

but do not touch. These unplanned quilts
are called *crazy*. Patches pieced with no
pattern—random except for intent.

The citi on the other side
of the river looks
like the citi on this side of the river.

Except I looked & someone looked back.

The Cloud 6

citi of alleys all *back*
behind the boulevards   alley-living
alleys of strays alleys of broken pipes
alleys of rich tenants & porters
alleys of runaways & unconquerables

                              reading Plato
by nite-light

citi in which the philosopher is not wanted
ideal citi
every citi where

            an hour cannot be spent more pleasantly
            than at Harry Hill's place on 25 East Houston Street:

brothel, towers
of shuffled papers, bodies
leaning toward dissolution in water

187 metal slugs or 2,200 gallons of A-1 jet fuel
which is more
dissolution

& amortizing memorials advertising grief
because telling always seems
the way

'cept the aliens ain't listening

citi of broken eyes navigating sidewalk cracks
because placing eyes back in the head means scalding fire

walking the dead man's route—
the Jornada del Muerto—Manhattan
Oppenheimer quoting the four-thousand-year-old
burn-your-eye-out texts:

De Civitate Dei

The Counterpane 6

There is no soup today.
Only bread. Without crust.
The impossible soft middle. The baker's hand
forming a long loaf rising like a body
& the skin, delicious & thin.
So much Adam's apple. Biting there.
We could live on such violations for centuries.
What did it mean? To snip the tenuous
threads of decorum, doing what we are told.
For how long?
Really? One day
there is no soup. The next
no bread—
your slim neck in my hands
the rising, the falling,
the split second between. That's the revolution.

The Cloud 7

she walks into the vestibule & leaves
a bomb meant for the ambassador

she walks into the vestibule & leaves an umbrella
I left at the table last night

which pattern chooses:
we'll see when they carry them out

I take the elevator down from 14E
step into open space

such saturated color, light, heat
flicking like a peony—the concentration

required to press my eyes against
her nape like a brave limb of birch

as she retreated into the kitchen
stepped back out again wet & on fire—

exiting the vestibule I
unfurl myself in the rain.

The Counterpane 7

Night of yackers
screamers & tight-lipped men
loose in their joints, their wet shadows
merging with old shadows
etched in the nineteenth-century sidewalk
—the membrane
between centuries, between sexes
thin as cobwebs:
nothing is in its place in a foreign citi.

I imagine the jib & jab of voices
out the open balcony window are not
about me thinking:

> *Q. What is the chief end of man?*
> *A. To glorify God, and to enjoy him forever.*

I'll never live that down. Fifty thimbles of bargain wine
each in nine concentric circles like planets orbiting the sun
or the *trepidation of the spheres:* communion.

I'll have another night of the gendered citi
short-sleeved men playing bass, dancing about
they do not know what since it hasn't
come to pass & already has many, many times.

Down wet night-lit streets come men
preened as ponies, hard-ons raging in their change pockets.
I've dreamt women sleep-faced, wearing pajamas
nestled on their sides
pregnant, pendant, moving inside.

I've dreamt nightmares of wounds & made moans
so loud I woke myself bellowing.
I somehow know what is coming—everything that follows
after the first Word

is what has to follow. I am one of these
men: I hear a man in a bar say *One*
& because he speaks I know just why I will die.
This is not because I'm proud.

I've dreamt he dapples me with whiskey
kisses then makes me sit on the Judas chair.

Tonight I'll dream a long dream of witness.

The Cloud 8

a topography of citi reveals
monuments to Babylon
ticking through the pavement—
glass, levers
slaves sleeping upright in dim corners
& tunnels sniffed by rats
stealing gold: pharaoh, mayor, architect
embalmer, saint

> atop the thwarting bull   Wall Street
> a ballerina *en pointe*
> a bronze man reading
> literature dumped from the Free Library
> a card catalog unwritten: occupied

blue horizontal lines, margin at the top
categorizing "citi"—

she *will go out in time, will go out*
      into time, hiding even her embers

I love you even as love refuses names
refuses to be named

because it is refugee
my sweet untold ballerina

Hassan.

The Counterpane 8

I chose that bouquet because the bee
had chosen it too. They were a farmer's flowers
& he had wrapped bands around the bunches
of yellow daisies, white clover, lavender, sweet pea

& something foreign to me, a spiky blue
alien flower, scentless head
a bit absurd, like an eclipse your teacher tells you
not to look at because it might blind.

The bee was busy liking it, a real
stinger & when I picked up the bunch
the bee followed along, stems much less robust
than I thought, slim & damp & lolling

in my hands, not grocery-store flowers bred stiff
for vases & lasting longer than natural—no.
In my palm I felt the hum of a life
I knew was not my own, the pulse of a kiss

placed at that hard bone, that notch
in your collar at the base of your throat. That
space I will pour myself into like I am melted
metal & will pool there & make a circle. That bee

its summer was there in my hand. That hot
eyeless sun flaring in the market
& I bring it home to you
yellow-black & alien blue absurd rubber-banded

farm-market love.
What we want—you, the bee
me, our hands over the stinger, making
our own sun run.

The Cloud 9

sometimes there is no edge—

just sheets of cloud
statistics underneath dying in each
other's arms, equations exchanging messages
on the backs of napkins & stars

sometimes there are no clouds—

nothing to cup hands around
color pure & tenderless, a message
readerless, the cobalt blue bed sheets after
you've gone, creaseless & empty

seven million drops walking citi
merging into cloud, falling, emptied, collected, rising
again into five-story walk-ups bleeding

mold the hundred-year storm left
documents signaling life
strewn about the apartment & underneath

the coffee cup a note you've left encoding
our next coming, our next Sutton Hoo
treasure sunk in Greenpoint Brooklyn muck—

our unearthing. sometimes genetics
explodes from alien directions
& Samar Hassan crouches

in corners. sometimes, there is
life where none is wanted—
but not in this house. I want

this & this & this, but not all
of these things want to be sewn
together. the pattern counter to plan is love.

The Counterpane 9

I

want to disavow because you have accused me of drinking too
    much
& I want to insist clear is blue
even though topsy is turvy & pour me another.

I

want to argue because my clock believes it is Daylight Savings
    Time
& in fact my time
contains nothing that will be saved.

I

too want to arm wrestle a French theorist
kiss him on the nose tip
just before I slam his arm into the counter
the one tattooed with the name of his last lover.

Eve, my sweet refugee
mother of all the losses
you've laid at my feet. I deserve them.
My Adam, myself, a man I'm just beginning to know
names wrongly.

It is all sound & strum & swaying hip
pressed onto hip, lap, breast, cradle & verve
slosh & bowl & drain & drip, not this & that
tyranny of the noun, rather pink & slow & hateful &
slick, vibrate & penultimate, precise, perambulations
around the garden

tea set in the basket, bottle of Pinot buried
under the rise, where all the slovenly wilderness rises up
to greet the mother & father of pain.

Make love to me! You great uncollected gathering flood.
You lightning storm.
You arm. You river. Port of fingers, neck & bones.

The Cloud 10

tonight the lights of citi come on for us
or at least this is the story
we tell isn't it because

the citis on the maps are never
the citis on the maps but a border that begs
crossing this night & that remorseless fence

that cold-wet water welcome
drowning in sight of land until *my friend*
drag me out & strangers in white gloves

pound water out the refugee's chest
turning over coughing dust
from tunnel-low below sedimentary

rock below pressure
below green water, oil tankers & cruise ships
swimmers embalmed in their yellow frog suits

fishing bodies out the river
below catatonic skyscrapers staring at their
beautiful skins winking in the river's mirror

below air & stars & void. we dug
another void below it all
& there were these souls where everyone knew

they might be hidden but no one
since the last god had thought to see
& then to us it seemed

the bores we made & the souls we had claimed
easing their way out the walls now
& into air

were the crest of it all, everything below
now rock now above then air
transfusing into air

all the ghosts in love with diggers' light.

The Counterpane 10

You are the ship & the sea
I had to leave I never
had to leave—at night the lights
scanning the beach
seemed a new world
& as I crawl between your thighs
it is, placing my nose in your hair
arms wrapped round your back
you are the wave between
me & the shore
I must swim to when the ship
founders, briny grind whirling
sirens & a song signaling
Stop—not
heeding the lieutenant's
glare. There's a matter of life & death
worth discussing
sure sure the lights are one
a new world
the same old world
I have grown to love
& will ravish
again
you citi
you nameless original (clear blue) smile. All
dissolution lingers too long—

then a yellow
Vespa flies by, two women on the machine
scissor, machine, spool
blade & rule

& we sew.

The Nothing

So as an artist of negative space he poured himself
into nothing & took breaks—sometimes weeks long—
recovering from the ardor of nothingness executed

with a jeweler's patience, though it was the rock-dust
grains powdering the cutting-room floor out of which
one day he would make a window, that clear pane

making (inside light) / (outside light) the birds
exterior, the children & multiplication tables interior.
Is this what it was? Division. Word. Splitting firmament.

The IED

Harun, come on, get into the house, it's grenading outside.

—Semezdin Mehmedinović, from *Sarajevo Blues*

The IED 1

Not because when I stepped on the trigger
you were watching that bee on a June morning hang

in the impossible air, not because you bent our curtain
against light the moment those electrons tripped the black hive

not, my love, because placing the burnt toast down
among the morning's calumnies, the crazed plates

was anything special. We all, I most of all, had done that.
You do that. There were children & I don't blame you.

Between the flash & the bang I imagined you unfolding
breakfast: glazed sausage, butter, tall orange sweating.

Again & again, I crawl into the skin I wake from.
Outside the window, you cut down

the offending bush, a beehive underground,
the queen disfigured, disconsolate, alone,

her children sequestered in cells. Before I heard the sting
I heard her coming.

She is full of the sperm of marked men—
fire tongue, stinging rain, collision.

Because I know you think it is your fault.
Because you know that I think it is mine.

The IED 2

Royal jelly   supersedure

                                      mouth-parts

larvae

          think boy

            cell

phone   calling   :

              Humvee fire

          swarm

steel plate   inside

slide in cells, in-

                side brain hole.   Some

where close by,

home

                                        detonation.

The IED 3

Not aprons
OR tablecloths ... sausages
... OR curtains sheered
against light
calumnies OR crazed plates
(like a map of oil pipelines
viewed from space) breakfast you were
making that tall ORange glass
sweat. Not ORder
OR love/ making pattern
could have stopped that bomb
from doing
its bomb thing.
That's what we make them fOR.

The IED 4

If I were fine
with you not coming back
I wouldn't have
burned my lunch, but now

crisped ham & cheese foozing
in molten yellow pools, the smoke alarm doing

what it does, I can't remember
the last time we kissed, not for sure—it could have been
over dinner:

exploded shells
pearls dispatched
legs broken
wet tongue of foreign sounds—*oeufs, jambon, fruits de mer*
—licking my ear. Somewhere

monks in their cowls skim the sea
salt just for you & the butcher asks
what cut you'll have
today. Please, bring home some tongue, a brain & yes

that heart.
This one's cooked too long
& I don't mean metaphorically.
Really, everything is burned
all the rooms smell like smoke
the onions have sprouted wings & even the vinegar
forgets its bitter. Come, enter

my mixing bowl, crack the eggs open wide
sharpen the knives
& strip the bed. Let's make a carnage, watch
it rise
in French.

Can't you hear this little sound
ticking down by the pilot light?
Make it stop.

The IED 5

Oregon 609, a hybrid berry
pedigree: loganberry-x-youngberry

each also a hybrid again
pedigree: raspberry-x-blackberry

& blackberry-x-dewberry, respectively.
Oregon 609, the noble olallieberry

resistant to verticillum wilt
half-father of the marionberry, also arrested

1990, re-elected 1992:
He May Not Be Perfect, But He's Perfect for D.C.

Transmogrified like the Chinook jargon
whence *olallie* issues, meaning *berry*, i.e. berry-berry

delicious, the slow anemia of language precipitated
by whites. 609 also the area code of Atlantic City

& Fort Dix, the Humvee M1114 a variant
of the M1113, "up-armored" after IEDs incinerated

too many or just macerated
this gamble, this hybrid, this man.

The IED 6

I of arms

I of no legs

      sweat-glazed pip of nightmare   iris   flower

you flesh   you stain   you planted   deep unaware

            egg

bed asleep under   irises

        irises asleep under

a pitched battle   dreaming   useless

    blued petals, blacked bulb.

Under the Sunday

sun, that flower bed   ragged

             wound

    a split tongue speaking
    aaalbuuumenn…

                              underground where close quiet wings
spread
rhizome
neural algae
blanket
breathing green zone   I wake earth-wet

blankets: rock cling.

        The wet in my mouth speaks stern, rod-straight.

    Will you assay biology? Will you assay

anthropology?

Leaf wrack
ruin sprouts

incredible   suns.

Yes, I'll away.

If that's what you want.

I'll away.

The IED 7

I cost one howling year & gods.
  And when Simon saw that through laying
  on of the apostles' hands the Holy Ghost was given,
  he offered them money. $1.3 trillion. Dear

I never thought I would cost this much.
  Nor would teleology: the price of laying on hands
  across your soft-wet belly, cost of babies
  checkpoints & Faust-black nightmares.

There were my legs entwined with yours & there
  congressional appropriations, untwining
  us from the same. Laying on hands...
  the papal forehead struck three times with a hammer.

Every rock of sand holds election. Tal Afar, Iraq: 18 Jan. 2005.
  When the bishops have it right, the smoke burns white.
  Eligo in Summum Pontificem Samar Hassan
  elected that night sprouting hair in the moonlight

constellations crackling the sedan's windshield when her
parents
  didn't stop at the darkened checkpoint, blood-patterning
  sidewalk where the photographer stalked, missing
  the olive private's weeping. Also Heidi Klum on *O'Brien*.

Mere democracy John Winthrop loathed, split
  the sodomizer's tongue, removed ears, thanked God
  for Election. Did not see, nor I, the sand mouth swallows
    speeding toward the hand sign signaling—*Stop*.

The IED 8

United in their refusal to stay in any one place
long, the roof pigeons coo me to sleep

—this strange bed in a strange city
making me feel more at home in my skin

than any room labeled home.

When I finish my bread & cheese at the café
the grackles move in to pick along the bricks

what I brush from my lap
delicious the last atom, at least to them.

Each meal is an exegesis of the *Book of Common Prayer*.

I want to pretend I don't know anyone
so you won't be there to disappoint

or maybe I want to forget those I do know
a man holding a hose in his trembling hand at 6:30 a.m.

The bricks swollen red.

The night poking its tongue in through the open
balcony door smells of other people's clothes

worn while doing things they won't tell.
At some point I wake & it is so quiet,

quiet like the void, like the day before there were bees.

The IED 9

The cutting board is no field of clover
        & I am no butcher
                but here we are, the rabbit

lying quiet, alone. Outside, the grass
        is dry, dust stuck to the windows & above
                the kitchen sink I can see a gray dove

begin its strut & coo, seeing another of its kind.
        When I run a finger from the back end
                toward the head, the fur parts

as if I have traced a seam in the earth
        though the effect retreats, the fur forgetting.
                The bones in its back resemble accordion

keys, its lungs, the billows & I think the last time
        I felt your skin, the bones across your back
                seemed to sing.

Now as the work begins, the dove flutters against
        the window, a white collar around its neck & I
                imagine its cocked head is symbolic

suggesting we have loved, it meant & the bird witnessed.
        Of course this is wrong. Of course everything
                is wrong, except the wound where I stuff

the bread, the apples & sew.

The Seam

Elska is not a word I expect you to know
but to someone in Iceland it is *love*, which is also
nothing I expect you to know, but means
etymologically there is steam under the earth
which may gush from its fissures any time of day or night
but often when no one is watching, not even the stars
caring either, their white light glowing
with an aloneness no one even knows to feel sad about.

Or maybe we would be floating there
like John White searching for his daughter
in our fragile barque just off the coast
& for the first time in a century we would see
the earth cracking its seam just a bit & the steam
would seem like the earth sighing
& the waves lapping over the gunwales
would feel less cold than they really are
& the mist like a
tongue like a
palm like an
aureole
like nothing after you've died would rain.

O! I know I go on
too much, all
gathered into the prow so that we might sink
but I want us to watch & imagine
in our human way

that the light is for us, when I know it is not, though at least
I am for you. Do you forgive me
my fecklessness
this indolence of too much & too many?
Inside, something touches my tongue that might
be a cloud or might also be just stone.

Always, this pressure under the earth must explode.

The Golden Venture

The mouth is a flooded machine

—Terrance Hayes, from *Lighthead*

The Golden Venture 1

The law demands a representative.

Asked to translate, I cannot translate myself.

My family came for the Gold Mountain (*Gam Saan*),
the California gold rush. When the earthquake destroyed
the records (there were no records), my grandfather became
a *Paper Son*. His slot was bought.

My father moved east to New York, found work, then west
to York, built his Wonderful Garden.

He said Americans can't eat enough Chinese.

The law demands a defendant understand the charges.

I barely know his dialect, this refugee, Shengqiao Chen. Not
Manchurian. Not Cantonese.

I was born in York, where the Underground Railroad ran.
Old York, I guess. The Lincoln Highway travels through town,
a ribbon tying two coasts.

The law demands *habeas corpus.*

The law demands a body to be prosecuted.

Messiah College in Mechanicsburg is my *alma mater*.
My degree is in English. China is my Epcot
where no one drowns and everyone buys souvenirs
signaling happiness.

The law makes demands of the body but never of the soul.

If interpretation is what you need, then that's more than
I was hired to provide.

The Golden Venture 2

I write in the report...

The *Golden Venture*
freighter
foundered
& Shengqiao Chen
was dragged to shore
eighteen-years-wet illegal
lungs split with salt—
off Queens
off Rockaway
off ship
ten jumped
over the side
into the screws

I would do it again
though
the water was cold
as was the beach
where nearly nude
girls
chests crushed
under latex hands
trying to restart hearts
were muled from Fujian
to America
vomiting sea.

I write in the margins...

what the screws do to you

what the lack of love does to you

every law does to you

every single law signaling

imagination failed

The Golden Venture 3

On my shelf, I never find the book I am looking for.

There is another, in a different language, with another spine.

Another way to cover what's underneath.

Alphabetization is a border fence holding out/in chaos.

Chinese has no tense.

Shengqiao Chen wants to learn.

The language of buying and selling.

I adjunct at the community college—English as a Second
    Language.

Proper use of the comma and the full stop.

Proper frame for an argument.

Proper attitude toward the opposing view.

An attitude toward anger.

Errors of article and agreement.

How to create great forts of words, impenetrable.

To experience.

Of the actual.

I choose a dictionary and *The Pilgrim's Progress.*

The proper use of the subjunctive requires a lifetime to learn.

And even then unnecessary.

This counterfactual condition.

The Golden Venture 4

CSX [*how tomorrow moves*]

train cars full of chemicals
through York

east toward Port Elizabeth
seagulls circling

toward Chengdu
where oysters drop from the rooftops

Foxconn built
into Apple's leaky

suicide nets [*how tomorrow moves*]

shift over or
about to begin

China that new old Eden
née America

rumbling out prison slits
[*how tomorrow moves*]

beside the railroad tracks
the mind's hand

lets go

The Golden Venture 5

I write in the report ...

Shengqiao Chen
watches the prison vigils
outside slitted windows
folding origami hands
from donated *GQ* mags—

my friend drag me out
the sea.

I write in the margins...

how many folds

right angles

shaped in laps

against rounded bars

form palm's meat

hand arching up the back

hand praying in upstate York

which buys the refugees

to populate the jails it built

awaiting the ships crashing

down on Far Rockaway to come

drowning to come

border crosser come

criminal walking five nights

against desert come

the profitable refugees

to York

my friend drag me out

come, the sea

The Golden Venture 6

"I had been watching the mockingbirds
on the ledge outside all night
& given up thinking
I was like them with their prepositions
signaling they knew their way
in, around, above, over, with & through.

There was just me here alone
so when the jailer—shaking keys
like a baby's rattle—told me to go, I thought
just knowing the door was open was enough
but when he threatened to walk away
I said, *Yes, I am coming*, gathered my papers
my origami hands
so that he did not think I loved his
blue eyes so much to stay
& ran.

The door was like that.
When I thought it would not open & nothing
could be on the other side, it did
& when I think it will never close, there is
someone there saying, *Hurry up*.

Here is a flower I folded for you
when I thought I would not see you again
& here are my empty hands."

The Golden Venture 7

What I translated...

I had dreamed you were the wide uncorrupted beach.
I had dreamed you were the heat
I had stolen away to find & you did not

toss me back, lucky Golden Venture
lucky me. You wore that dress (I did not
care) & your hair in its impossible tangles opened
just for me, parolee.

I thought I had the choice to love, stupid
me. The ship, it chose & the sea.

The moonlight does not care if I drown or you

if I drink seawater or clouds, night
or you, waiting in your dimly lit room
rocked by storms for me
the bed rising & falling with the sea

choosing
refugee me.

The Golden Venture 8

What the papers say...

Death of the freighter
Golden Venture towed
down off Boca Raton
mouth of stones
mouth of ship's bones
rats caught in the trap

the Coast Guard
the water cannons
making her sink
making her grave
marking her a site
for divers
swimming through her belly

within sight of the Gold Coast

laid to rest

an artificial reef

I am not dead

inked
in the skin's creases
washed away

What my dreams say...

who does not want
a new land
new city
clean
like god
smelling *Tree*
        the first time?

        that is what you are to me
        U(S)

clear sea unctuous lover
contraband. citi
screams its all-too-human
arms
& Shengqiao Chen
double-helical
human
pinches dumplings
along Brooklyn Battery
singing subways

& Sunando Sen
great underground tunnels
crossing & recrossing
        exiting
        everywhere.

The Drowned

The pool refused the clouds
in such a way that we were never

angry at the pool, since it was so ripe
with its own anger that our intentions

were just refracted, scattered into the trees
to rest there like crows huddled against the wind.

Children's toys adrift, choked with water,
the miniature cabin boy glued to his master's

porthole, screaming, *The cherries! The cherries!*
would freeze there like that forever

since no one, as the storm moved in
had thought to let poor Pip out.

Fury was like that: whipped to froth
without sextant, log or chart, daring one

moment of a bird's song to fill the silence:
breaking the animal's neck. *Oh, my master*

my slave, my lover, come back! Your poor
Pip needs you, promises to tell you all.

No answer. The water just a dumb thing
& we, having turned into the wind.

The Cloud 1

In 2012, Hurricane Sandy destroyed thousands of barrels of DNA
evidence warehoused in Brooklyn by the NYPD.

In 1939, a burial ship containing the regalia of an Anglo-Saxon king
was unearthed in Sutton Hoo, England. Its contents are on view in
the British Museum.

The Counterpane 1

Quilt patterns are often named. Some patterns served as messages
for runaway slaves along the Underground Railroad.

The Cloud 2

The Arecibo message was delivered into space via radio telescope in
1974. The Wow! message is the name ascribed to a signal received
by a radio telescope working on the SETI project in 1977 and
suspected to be of extra-terrestrial origin. It was only "heard" once
and never since.

The Cloud 3

Samar Hassan survived her parents when their car was raked
with bullets at an American checkpoint in 2005. A photo of her
immediately taken afterward, by Chris Hondros, is one of the few
iconic images to emerge from the war.

The Counterpane 3

This poem was inspired by the Post-WW II Japanese art collective, Gutai, which was featured at the Guggenheim Museum in 2013.

The Cloud 4

Sunando Sen was killed on Dec. 27, 2012, when he was pushed under the No. 7 train in Queens. The poem, however, adopts a different train line and location. The quote is from Erika Menendez, who was charged with second-degree murder in the attack.

The Cloud 7

The line "we'll see them when they carry them out" is from Wisława Szymborska's poem "The Terrorist, He's Watching."

The Counterpane 7

The Question and Answer are quoted from the *Westminster Shorter Catechism*.

The Cloud 8

In Zuccotti Park, the Occupy Wall Street movement established a Free Library.

The lines "will go out in time, will go out/into time, hiding even her embers" are from Robert Duncan's poem " Tribal Memories: Passages 1," though my quote does substitute "her" for "its."

The IED 7

The poem's opening line, "I cost one howling year & gods," takes one word from each line, in order, of the first seven lines of Pounds' Canto III.

The biblical quote is from Acts 8:18.

In 2011, the Congressional Research Service estimated that Congress had appropriated $1.3 trillion additional dollars to the Department of Defense to fight the wars in Iraq and Afghanistan.

The Seam

John White was an artist who became the governor of the first English colony in America, on Roanoke Island. At some point, around 1590, while White was in England, the colonists, including his daughter and granddaughter, vanished. He searched for but never found them again.

The Golden Venture

The freighter *Golden Venture* ran aground off Rockaway Beach, Queens in 1993, carrying nearly three hundred undocumented immigrants from China. Ten died trying to reach shore. Many were jailed for years in York, Pennsylvania as their asylum claims worked through the legal system. Those who were paroled are still without final legal status.

ALICE JAMES BOOKS has been publishing poetry since 1973. The press was founded in Boston, Massachusetts as a cooperative wherein authors performed the day-to-day undertakings of the press. This collaborative element remains viable even today, as authors who publish with the press are also invited to become members of the editorial board and participate in editorial decisions at the press. The editorial board selects manuscripts for publication via the press's annual, national competition, the Alice James Award. Alice James Books seeks to support women writers and was named for Alice James, sister to William and Henry, whose extraordinary gift for writing went unrecognized during her lifetime.

DESIGNED BY MIKE BURTON

PRINTED BY THOMSON-SHORE